COMMANDMENTS

OTHER BOOKS BY JACKIE WILLS

Powder Tower
Arc Publications, 1995

Party
Leviathan, 2000

Fever Tree
Arc Publications 2003

COMMANDMENTS
Jackie Wills

PUBLICATIONS
2007

Published by Arc Publications
Nanholme Mill, Shaw Wood Road
Todmorden OL14 6DA, UK
www.arcpublications.co.uk

ISBN-13: 978 1904614 00 5

ACKNOWLEDGEMENTS:
Poems in this book have previously appeared in:
*The Book of Hopes and Dreams, Equinox, The Frogmore Papers,
Hard Times, London International Animation Festival 2006,
Nth Position, The North, The Poetry Paper, Poetry Review,
The Rialto, Seam* and *Warwick Review.*
The author is grateful to
The Poetry Trust for a residency at the
Aldeburgh Poetry Festival in 2004, The South,
to I⎯⎯⎯⎯⎯⎯⎯⎯⎯⎯⎯⎯⎯⎯2005,

She a⎯⎯⎯⎯⎯⎯ wishes to thank M⎯⎯⎯⎯⎯⎯⎯⎯⎯lmonte,
Bre⎯⎯⎯ham Crory, A⎯⎯stair Cre⎯⎯⎯⎯, Jane Fordham,
Jud⎯⎯⎯ Kazantzis, Tim Liardet an⎯⎯ Catherine Mellor.

The Publishers acknowledge financial
assistance from ACE Yorkshire

ROTATION
STOCK

Editor for the UK and Ireland: Jo Shapcott

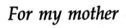

For my mother

Contents

PART I

The birds sing about water

The birds carry a river,
their chorus in my throat,
in the dry spring I walk to,
useless tap, slashed water tank.
I stand in a metal tub with a flannel
waiting for them to fill it drop by drop.

The birds carry a river,
lifted from its source, pulled over
this valley to water mangoes, lychees, tea.
It runs over stones in their beaks.
They shake waterfalls from their wings
drumming pools deeper than feet can reach.

The birds carry a river,
sing until Mashau's roads are rapids.
Fistfuls of pebbles slam on the zozo's
tin roof. Children lay down bottles,
paint buckets, cans. The malachite
kingfisher shows us how to dive.

The birds carry a river
to a priest growling his prayers,
past mercenaries at the plantation gates.
If they could hide it, lay pipes for it
they would, but the birds carry a river
litre by heavy litre on their heads.

Honour one god

Honour the god that comes to you
dividing marigold seedlings
scattered among feverfew,
pulling weeds from a row of new leeks,
fragile as cobwebs – a cat, maybe,
lying on an abandoned plot
as dandelions balloon into fluff
and the orange slow-worm you disturb
under a slice of elm, a wren,
busy as your mother, a starling,
opinionated as your father –
a god that can't be summoned
or charmed, like rain.

Love song for Fidel Castro

They've started a tight salsa
when Elisa strolls on, hips round as a drum.

Her band whoops, edges up the percussion
and the bass whips her calves.

She looks at each woman, remembering
how she brought them together,

their babies now workers, mothers,
or fathers, grins at the years they display

in their breasts, waists and eyes,
one thousand, three hundred and three.

She nods to Aleida on congas holding rivers
in her palms and Mathilda, the oldest,

on rhythm guitar, playing just as she's waited
in a chair by the door, night after night all her life.

Elisa turns to the room, finds the President's table,
puts a mike to her mouth.

"For this man tonight, twenty lovers," she jokes
and her eyes won't leave as she sings

of sun in the citrus, Batista,
all the sweat and fists in the wind,

of a child in a cellar, paths through the cane,
the wings on every island's shoulder blades.

She sings of the speeches scrolled in his pockets,
of Angola, Mandela, his friend.

She sings of Havana, how it still burns
on maps of the world,

of Martí's white rose and an exile's return
to the Island of Youth.

Then she picks up the claves and the crowd
shines the floor with its footwork,

as they dance the way heat breaks
the line of a road, each beat and bell of the salsa,

a gasp in the hand.

Don't make idols

Who are you kidding? Just watch me bow
to a colour photocopy of the prophet,
turn on a switch to light up that plastic
virgin from a church supplier. I'll queue
in any unknown cathedral to rub a relic,
run my thumb over a martyr's smile.
It's like holy water – you do it for luck.
Yes, I'd leave a bloody tampon at a shrine,
burn candles for my Catholic father.
I have a collection of devils whittled
from bone and at the garden centre,
found a Buddha's face in concrete. Next
on my list's a Chinese Christ. I've cast
my enemy as a Valkyrie in plaster,
put Shiva on my best friend's wedding cake.
I like a trickster best, or feathered snake.

The other woman

She texts him the entire Kama Sutra,
promising to fork French patisserie
into his mouth, sweet with custard.

The other woman's like new neighbours
erecting a six foot fence, who don't tell you
builders will be drilling on Saturday morning.

Alert and supple as a contortionist,
she can stretch a stilletoed leg to the ceiling,
write her name with the heel.

The other woman can summon fog
out of a clear sky, dilate her pupils
so wide a man will fall in, gratefully.

She'll try and get into bed with you, too,
lift a corner of your duvet,
to stake a claim on the mattress.

The other woman waits until your parking space
is free, then nips in with her Renault Clio,
the neat boot stuffed with underwear.

Don't take my name in vain

What makes you think an alphabet will do,
or curls of gold, elaborate calligraphy?

Your hymns, chants, songs, satisfy
only yourselves. Even your science tries

to mimic me. Your stories sanctify
God, Allah, Yahwe,

a line of men you try to conjure
with incense, honour with fasts.

You repeat my name along the chapel
corridor, bow to me five times a day.

You meditate for hours under a beech
tree, light candles incessantly.

Zeus, Buddha, Odin. Every name
you've given me is wrong.

Impala
(for Mrisi)

"Pimp," he calls from the car window
at the buck with a herd of female impala
and fawns in the shade of a thorn tree.

My 12-year-old son sees MTV, a rapper
with his entourage of teenage girls.
He's right. They belong here,
beautiful, sleek, toned, alert, every hair
on their skin tuned to the wind,
to scorpions moving through the bush,

to the Bateleur eagle circling overhead
as the sun sets and a lioness roars,
frightening the dry river into a streaked sky.

They hear the squirrel's shock
when a kingfisher spears its thigh,
the rains so late, fish might as well be stars,

they feel the wind change, the pollen it carries,
the rumble of people on the move, their absence
at night corralled in shelters. They taste
the missing rain in dry savannah.

Even on street corners,
young men smell meadows
stretching over the horizon,
as on the swings, smoking teenagers
recall endless beaches

and in the flux of evening,
look to the edge of the city –
to the lioness washing her cubs,
crickets rattling the heat of tomorrow

when elephants on the move into the hills
will rip up the bush, bathe in clouds of dust.

Day of rest

The order comes: "Down tools."
You stop driving buses, lock the tills.
Guides leave the Taj Mahal,
Pyramids. Ski-lifts hang over glaciers.
In markets, all you hear is flies –
there's no-one underground, no planes,
no money moves. TVs show blue lagoons
to a soundtrack of wind. Food's eaten raw.
Your tongue remembers the taste of blood,
your hand how an apple gives as you pull
it from a tree. Dancing returns to empty
spaces the way a cactus blooms.
You watch a wren, look up to the sky
you fell from. You become the greeting
of a Venda woman: "Ah," a slow exhalation.

Girls

(for Giya)

A hen night, but not a hen night
a line of 11-year-old girls
in fairy wings, net skirts
arms round one another
running to the pier
on a Saturday night
crowds parting outside bars
men looking twice
once in shame
women laughing
at what they were
girls scattering the boozers
Big Issue sellers
a meat wagon
calling "I love you" back
bouncers open-mouthed
at the noise
stag nights halted
as they stumble, badged up
"Flirt", "Ready & waiting"
but not for these girls
heading towards the wild mouse
water ride, helter skelter
every illuminated thrill
mirrored in a sea
now full of them.

Honour your father and mother

My father with willow trees curving
over a stream – a tunnel where silence
bends into earth and swans
stretch ancient wings.

My mother with marigolds, neat
as the rhythm of a sewing machine
stitching our garden to pine woods,
cutting trousers from the sky.

Alphabetic

(the A to Z of birth)

Here's baby A, swaddled in a bin-liner
dressed in a sweatshirt his mother wore,
bouncy B's exit was recorded on camera,
her head clamped in the beak of a stork.

Clever mite C dropped from an ambulance
in the hospital car-park, name on a tag,
and D's the famous embarrassment
left at Victoria station, in a handbag.

E is the bundle a postman delivered,
F, bought from an Argos catalogue,
this little girl, G, was made in a factory
and H reared by rabbits, found by a dog.

Brothers I and J emerged from a toilet,
and cheeky K arrived with the chips.
L was grown on daddy's allotment –
as you can see from the soil on her lips.

Look at M, the cat brought him home,
N, fat slug, and her gooseberry bush...
O, a surprise, was delivered by aliens
and P raised from clay by Prometheus.

Now, Q, the original test-tube baby...
R, a beauty, is cloned from her mum.
Watch out for S, born on a ski-slope,
and mythical T, the size of a thumb.

An addict, already, U screams for crack,
V is damned by original sin.
W's winched from floods in Mozambique
and X is cut from the guts of her twin.

That's twenty-four, just two more to come.
Out of the waves, swims foam baby, Y.
Arms raised, she leads to the very last one –
Z, a star made of darkness in a distant sky.

Don't kill

Clouds pass over in bands,
the moon rises red,
occupies the sky, draws
the fire nearer,
colours the lake
hiding in dry mountains,
fed by a stream
carrying the screams
of children captive in drums.
The water won't mix.
The lake silences them.
"Sssh," it whispers, "they'll hear."
But the lake's far from anywhere.

Mind museum

Made of glass, the museum overlooks the Pacific
from a contaminated atoll, an architect's joke.

I came to the island as a goose blown off course by the wind.
In the distance, a domed roof reflecting the sun

and as I approached down a track, was compelled to go in.
At first, I saw only the sign: *Entry is free by appointment.*

There was no one around. I looked for a bell, wondered
if I should call, stood watching the ocean.

She seemed to walk out of the glass, my reflection.
"Jan, I'm your guide. Follow me." We began on the ground

floor with a traveller's mind, narrowed to a lens.
He'd transported the Rialto to the Pyrenees.

Then she showed me a pinhole drilled into the sky.
Through it I saw Niagara crash down a slide. "An agoraphobic,"

she said. I watched as the path to a door was transformed –
a dirt road through mountains. I looked for the track I'd walked up,

unsure if I was inside or out. It was gone. "We have minds
preserved in the thought they died with," she told me.

By then, though, I'd seen stairs in a corner where before
there was nothing. As I climbed, each step below disappeared.

The room we entered glowed like an equatorial night sky.
"These are living minds. The first simulation is birth."

Jan pointed to a console. "You can prompt the birth mind to dream,
images will appear on the screen." I watched the mind root

for shapes, stagger from the womb to the street and call.
Next, in a tube, like gloop, was a mind as it wandered

to rain on a window, a red spot on the cashier's nose. Jan
showed me a curtain, behind it the dark of mind without speech.

There was a crescent so sharp, it earned a place on the flag.
I heard seas whisper to mapmakers, urge children to draw them.

Outside, by a fire stood mind without sight: an elderly man
with a bucket of water. In it he'd captured the sun, the horizon.

In turn, he pointed to mind without language. And there it was,
worm-mottled, under a hydrangea after last night's storm.

It brought autumn down sticky with mud, tasted of winter.
Jan took my arm then and I felt her concern.

I heard keening women knock on a door, penitents' chains,
Sparta's boys scream. "The mind distorting finds its own people,"

she warned, keeping hold of my arm, and there was a father,
a funeral, a family turned to nothing. He was calculating

27

the ground a flayed skin could cover, knees swollen
with rags. A fence whined, a chimney beat time to the wind.

I felt like I knew him but there was a window between us
and more so I let Jan lead. She logged onto the web

and there was the mind altered forever by Google: motorway minds,
washing machine minds. I could have been lost for hours but I laughed

and the keyboard released a spray of the mind's essence
before reason: the bee-sting, my own ungrown wings. That was it.

"We hope you'll return," and she'd gone. I was left where I entered,
recognising nothing but instructions engraved on a door:

*Exit by the lake, visualise the lotus throne, the mind's ten
directions, its fifty billion-storeyed pavilions.*

Don't commit adultery

In a hotel room, rented flat, a friend's place, beach,
car, caravan, your own bed, his or her bed,
the children's beds, with dogs, that guy from the Red
House, your boss, on a motorbike, in a coach,

wearing that old leather jacket, after a cricket
match, in a tent, while your second child is being born,
watching a famous boxer do press ups in the gym,
while your first child is being born, after 10 shots

of Greek brandy, with someone who writes fan mail,
with your therapist, the priest, manager or director,
wife of your best friend, while your wife is having a
hysterectomy, because she has thrush, piles,

with your son's teacher, when your husband's in a coma,
with your son's girlfriend, in the Pussycat Club, with a lap
dancer, while smoking a cigar or reading the latest crap
crime fiction, contemplating Escher's prints in the Alhambra,

while your partner's leaving a message on your mobile,
by e-mail, live webcam, wearing stiletto heels, while your wife
is undergoing radiotherapy, while flying a plane, in Fife
station, with a doctor, over the baby listening device.

Women of affairs

They're like eyes stuck to my windows,
know everything about me –
my bra size, when I was last in hospital.

The eyes skin me like a doe
I saw hanging in a woodshed
in Dunsfold. There'd been a murder.

The doe was hung by her legs,
head down. This is what these eyes
do to me, peering in through the glass.

Don't steal

This thief knows the path
through the graveyard, vault over our wall.

> She steals the Sunday doing nothing.
> She steals the fingers from my arm.

Her dropped phone, Quaker mother,
Biblical name.

> She steals the gasp, night-time story.
> She steals the click of the front door.

I've talked to her,
danced behind her, not knowing.

> She steals the wine, late night chocolate.
> She steals my face from the mirror.

A colony of swans left a featherbed
beside the Kennet. She shat in it.

A life of sin

Only old people, over 50, remember
original sin, like the walnut-lined cars
we rode in without seatbelts or airbags,
unreliable in cold, wet winters.

Swollen with sin from birth, replete,
overfed, our lives were exhausted with sin,
expanded, flooded, pumpkin-big with sin.
So many to invent, so many never confessed.

The commonest? Theft, impersonating
the horizon with its simple arguments
maybe, or lust, balanced in a palm,
comfortable as a long-handled spoon.

Don't lie

The crow,
cruising a cliff for chicks,
doesn't lie.

Priest-black. I watch it
against the chalk,
scouting for soft beaks.

On a pebble beach,
a June sea raises
goosebumps on my legs

as I float in the space
a mirage might inhabit
between earth and sky.

I'm weightless
among the missing hours
I discover there.

Her promises

All the obvious ones,
a hanging garden of Babylon,
the plains of heaven
scented with neroli.

They gather outside
forming a queue around the block
as if they're auditioning
for a part as a child star,

rehearsing their lines:
no questions, no vows,
no tears or taboos,
no relatives, no periods,

no headaches or holidays
in Spain. She promises him
faithfully he'll never
have to meet her friends.

Don't covet your neighbour's goods

Desire the crystal drop
of a chandelier,
Swiss Army knife,
for the marks they make
on walls, the pauses
they offer. Memory's enough.
Pick clay from the lost city
you'll become. Watch
how sea turns mahogany
to driftwood, restores metal
to sand. What cloud wishes
for snow, heavier rain?

Leaving it to the cuckoos

When a road falls down a mountain,
when bits of it crumble till it's no longer a road
but a balancing act, when a road cracks
or a middle section, in the dip, is so worn
there's nothing to keep it flat;
when a road can't bear the weight
of a truck or car, when the rock overhang
pushes wheels further to the edge,
when the edge wants to meet the overhang,
the only way to the house is over the mountain –
a trek through gorse, bracken and bilberries,
quartz-lined rock, slate, scree and sand
where ravens hop and larks burst from pebbles,
where the cuckoos call near Echo Rock
filling the valley to the sea, their song bigger than lakes,
mocking all of us who imagine cars, books
or waterwheels will be enough. Once the mountain-side
owns the road, has pulled it into the pass
with a bumper and rusting exhaust, the house
with its feral cat and empty kennels
will be abandoned to the cuckoos.

The islands

Here light expands the tunnel you've become.
A big sky always takes you in.
There's no one but the Hebrides chattering,
a stone leans towards another; a lover listening.
Birds don't care if you live or die.
Here a cloud tries to be a mountain-top.
Colours need water and you are water.
Silent Steinways replay each odd and even year.
One day an Annunciation will happen.

Face

In my daughter's smile is the gap
passed along Welsh valleys and Cornish cliffs
where a view of the Atlantic narrows to a gasp.

Pearl's there too and a Venda great-grandmother's
gentle welcome. Wound in her curls are paths
between ancient trees and words she can't speak.

My grandfather crouches in my son's middle name,
peeling his nightly orange, a drill in his hand.
He wears a dentist's coat, pumps the chair with his foot.

His father, Edwardian, pulls back my son's shoulders
but my mother claims the hairline.
In his dimples, Aubrey, dead before time.

My first name makes only one appearance
in the family. It belongs to the iconic wife
of a president, style of sunglasses, a magazine.

It's rooted in the decade I became a teenager,
when the world jumped into a Sunbeam Talbot,
pulled down the top and tried to find itself.

My mother's half

stretched themselves into trade winds.
From a boxer and cobbler with Dublin in them
my mother's half hid in Midlands smog
and listened to bombs flatten Coventry,
their faces lit by night fires.

My mother's half stayed away.
No Xmas cards or grandfather,
no phone calls from uncles, no family portraits.

My mother's half
was the unexplored side of a planet
never warmed by a star.
My mother was motherless.
The only girl in a tribe of men.

My mother's half and father's half didn't meet.
She arrived like an anonymous donation,
historyless. Somewhere in my mother's half
are horses, forests, hordes of cousins
I might pass in the street tomorrow.
There are marriages, funerals she has no dates for.

Like the ghost stories she tells on walks,
my mother's half is mysterious.
Who gave her green fingers, thick, curly hair?

My mother ate raw swede to fill her stomach
empty from rationing, ran away at eleven,
island-hopping, ferry to train.

My mother made a garden for her half,
where it joined other lost halves:
children who spend lives
reconstructing a father's face
from plugs of wood, fistfuls of clay.

Her other half joins secret families, too,
for imagined anniversaries.
She'll never know, but in that place
maybe, her missing half glows.

The me who drinks too much

Who'd resist Chablis the colour of tourmaline
in a purse at my father's house,
stamped with the name of a shop in Rio?
And Morgon. See yourself in its velvet room,
old leather chairs and faded maroon curtains
releasing ancient suitcases, patchouli and roses.
With this red I need books and endless talk,
garlicky tomato sauce, fired with chilli,
and a map of the world to plot a course.
There's no chance of sleep until light comes;
then rooms smelling of smoke and candlewax
can shut their doors. Daytime trains,
the neighbours' radio, will soothe me to sleep;
the red and the black will finally let me go.

Her fangs, her horns

She's become a teenager's graffiti
on the underground, a model
defaced with indelible beard;
her cloven hooves stamping tracks
in our muddy garden path.
She's left her spoor for us to find,
no incense can mask her scent
in the kitchen each morning.

And he's become her drum,
each surface shuddering
until glasses, books, a vase, totter
to the floor and wind-chimes
hanging in the rosemary
outside the back door signal
she's here again, her heavy breath
almost rearranging the night air.

The me who's a wish

Let me be the eye,
a lens hanging
from each stalk
in which an ocean waits,
drawn down
from a cloudless sky.
Swimming in me
is the sun, a curve
of undiscovered chants.

Ravine

The python swam all day
through the bottomless sky,
pulled the moon

up the valley and tied it
by the Levubu river
to shine on us all by the fire.

What a moon he hung over
that ravine where a choir hid,
practising laments.

What a moon he hung over
those weeks as your secret
daughter grew.

"Talk," the python says.
Your daughter's hiding
in her mother behind the shack

and night after night, the bush baby
screams in the woods,
trying to tell us she's there.

Wise woman, throw your shells.
This girl has to stitch herself
into the days to come.

The me who's a mother

"Watch me dance." How my back bends
kneeling to tie a shoe, arms stretch
to a pavement with bags, how I tense
anticipating a fall, step forward to catch
a ball. My two children repeat each "bloody hell".
There's so much to pass on: stories lost
along the way, the taste of pineapple
sound of gamelan, a Welsh miners' chorus.
I show them a swan walk on water as it lands,
a child acrobat dancing on his hands,
a brown river break its banks. I conceal
how I pine for them already, let them go
until the radius they describe around me
is the world: equator, two tropics, two poles.

Inured

His phone is the shadow
part of him she lives in,

under the letter L,
flat as a Sim card.

She spins between base stations
day and night.

I wonder if she'll ever escape
from the flip up mouthpiece

he folds down on her,
what it takes to survive

in that ironed-out place,
so sensitive to water,

the deadly mineral
she's walled up with,

the war for it,
the radiation,

and if she thinks of me
when he refuses to answer.

The me who won't be civilised

climbs out of fields, blue
in the distance, hides waterfalls
and loose stones. I'm a cliff,
the place clouds descend to,
made from earth shifting,
continents moving, seas forming.
I want my people back,
the ones who moved away,
milked cows. Give them to me.
I'll show them caves, snakes,
massive spiders, all the wild
fruit they can eat, not this wheat
they grind and pummel into bread.

Pieces of her

She's bindweed,
finding a stem first,
spreading into the *weigela*
until it looks like her.

I find her wherever I dig,
bone-white root fragments,
convolvulus – so familiar
with hedges, waste ground.

How mundane she is
covering the lily, climbing into
the low apple tree,
stunting new leeks.

But how she changes everything.
No fruit left by July,
the garden smothered
by a rampant green duvet.

Waiting

Where's my lover?

Not in the wind
banging on windows,
or clouds,
so slow
to turn pink and grey.

If I whistle
will he rush to me
over the Downs?

I long for Antarctica's days,
endless
as queues for bread,
squatters reclaiming wasteland.

Children wait for kisses,
mothers stand by graves
until the Resurrection.

In three hours,
I meet them all.

Together
we stare
into the next minute

hoping land and light
will break our fall
and cushion us, soft as silt.

Her sleepless nights

Giant airbags expand to fill her room,
set off by beer cans kicked against a fence,
fireworks for a distant birthday, a phone.
For every night of sleep or sleeplessness
takes the form of the day it ends. Airbags,
soft, suffocating, press her on a desk –
a pen begins altering her face, pins
stab into every letter of her name.

Her worries refuse a shape. She tries ants,
baby shoes, paces the eroded banks
of that river, past docile, long-horned cows.
Hens scatter as she reaches the shack door.
All she feels is the same absence of air,
a tropical night, filled with wings and claws.

Fire-eater

He's explaining his route south, to the Pyrenees,
cooking broad beans on an open fire.
A 10-day round trip. He wants to take me
to bed before he goes. It's in the corner, high
as my grandfather's. On the table are tomatoes
still smelling of the stem. The map's laid out,
our hair touches as we lean over it; he shows
me Puy-de-Dôme, the road he'll take from Nantes.

The journey passes between us. He guides
me to the men I've known. One describes my hand,
how my breath smells of smoke, another my thigh.
The third holds a black moon I shed from a sequined
dress. The last recalls the tip of my shoe, green
fingernails, as I feed him segments of tangerine.

Letter

Her letter's disturbing the sorting office,
its mortgage applications, insurance forms.

Brown ink on a thick cream envelope.
Is there a hand squashed inside, a pelt?

The postman feels it move in his bag, restless,
but it calms as he meanders the streets,

walked back to sleep so an older script,
fainter, can appear on paper turned to vellum,

tracing four ponies emerging from woods.
So much she has yet to tell him.

The oldest kingdom

When they meet at the border
of the oldest kingdom
the checkpoint will be guarded
by an elderly woman
holding a glass of mead,
salty mountain cheese.

She'll inspect the two of them,
trace the lines of their palms.
For this is the border of longing.

As they cross, the old gods will cheer,
rustle bushes and spin the moon,
laugh loud and deep enough
to draw the Amazon
back from the sea to its source.

At that moment they'll know
the word for love
in every language ever spoken.

It'll never be repeated,
they won't remember.

But sometimes
it'll be as if a singing bowl
was struck in a cavern
where herds of deer, bison
and horses rear out of the wall.

Desire

First the heartbeat,
rain on mud,
next the cow in pain all night,
a river in flood,
a fox round the bins,
the groan of birth,
a cliff of larks,
the wind.

Then a deep "hello,"
her name,
in the moment
a heron's wing
might touch
a morning sea.

It belongs to hoof-beats
on turf,
lifts a bottle of Merlot,
says "now then,"
waiting.

A hello
she never wants to stop answering.
A hello she walks, swims,
sleeps and wakes with.
It fills and empties her.

Crawling on pebbles

When she played her arrival on the metal stairs
a fleet of fishermen began loading nets.

When his eyes closed the door of the house
the Harmattan gathered Saharan dust.

When coins fell out of his shirt pocket
a cathedral of sequoias grew in a forest.

When his tongue stopped her saying a word
greengages sobbed from an orchard.

When she struggled with his buckle, kneeling,
she was crawling on pebbles in the surf.

When she fitted her palm on his shoulder
a stream disappeared underground

PART II

For a path of 12 circular stepping stones

Between footsteps, here meets there
earth and water find fire, air
between footsteps, night stays blue
a meadow climbs to the new moon
between footsteps, mountains kiss
Venus appears, a sail vanishes
between footsteps, a blackbird calls
seconds touch before they fall
between footsteps, a thought spins
the shoe meets its missing twin
between footsteps a river flows
towards the sea, the dark below.

Towards the sea, the dark below
between footsteps a river flows
the shoe meets its missing twin
between footsteps, a thought spins
seconds touch before they fall
between footsteps, a blackbird calls
Venus appears, a sail vanishes
between footsteps, mountains kiss
a meadow climbs to the new moon
between footsteps, night stays blue
earth and water find fire, air
between footsteps, here meets there.

Concerns of a mature woman

I suspect moods break out like racehorses.
I probe the meaning of "atrophy," whispered
by a consultant gynaecologist, escape
to a leaky shed to boil water on camping gas
among cobwebs lumpy with velvet cocoons, breathe
herbal infusions from my collection of teapots.
I stop using scales or paper patterns,
save jam-jar lids and the postman's rubber bands.

I want a year in a Carmelite convent
to re-emerge as a flood plain, grow layers of silt
where Canada geese gather. I'll taste of salt,
a flat sky and jetties. I'll inhabit silence,
lure bevies of swans to bends in the river
while it swells with winter, breaks its banks.

How long could you stretch a summer?

The apple tree tricked
into a double blossoming,
garlic dormant for lack of frost –
a year swollen with squash,
a year of raspberries. Imagine
their soft give, your fingertips
stained permanently as they return
the earth to you day after day.
How long could you spin yourself
into talk on terraces,
rest hands on open windows,
imprint yourself on a lawn
until you're a pale green shadow,
wrists and neck white with chains?
Would it be like keeping a life
when it wants to leave? A body deep
into the tunnels of childhood again,
cats' cradles carefully hung with dew.

Salmonskin coat

When she stretches out of her hunch,
stands back, fingers blunt with thimbles,
a needle in the corner of her mouth,

looks at it draped on my shoulders,
flapping unadorned and unstitched,
she could be squinting for a child in snow.

She knows the diameter of my wrist,
the length of my back and forearm,
the fall to my knee, the size of my bust.

She knows panels speak to each other,
the shape of a soul, what arms need.
She hides herself in the seams.

When she asks what colours
I want embroidered on the back,
she warns it'll swim away with me,

this coat of sixty salmon skins –
arch into the Lower Amur river,
a run of sinew, scales and silk.

Theatre

The sky was heating up
I could hardly breathe.

What with swallows
diving through it like kids in a pool,
all screaming.

What with the moon
ready to burst like a sack of water.

What with pavements
peeling themselves from earth,
hanging just above, just below,
a tangle of magic carpets.

What with people
fanning, spraying, drinking
slower and slower
until, work, what was that?

It seemed the sky was about to break
over every country in the world
where people gathered,

over palaces and chapels
made for popes, preachers,
prophets, saints,

for benediction, meditation, glory.

First the thunder a long way off
like a barrow wheeled over cobbles
around the corner,
a drum not played but rolled.

Next, cameras, matches,
the seam revealed.

Over savannahs sky played
like a boy striking a hammer
against metal dripping petrol.

Over the poles sky raged –
that they could be so cold,
that they could make shapes
sky never dreamed of,
that they could mimic earth.

Over cities sky was art.
It touched all there was on earth

the Algerian sweeping a courtyard,
the Malian digging a road,
the gardener from Poland,
her hands in the soil.

A day in November

Sealed in Devon's grey mass,
tors rising and falling
beyond the sea glare,
a field sown with every detail

of a Cessna, its markings,
fuel tanks, when it took off,
route from the airfield,
the time a splutter was noted.

That morning the sun replayed
everything sighed in the dark
and I watched the day
lay out its ambushed dead.

Appeasement

Today the wind hammers its strings
and the beach returns its crushing reply.

Between these chalk cliffs and surf
are so many shades of white.

Perhaps in the doctrine of the tideline,
among cuttlefish and bladderwrack,

brush-heads and shampoo bottles
is the offering you're looking for.

Whitehawk

The boy's found curled like a foetus
by the golf club, disturbed by a JCB,
his skull smashed, alone, facing north.
Sixteen, maybe, his feet to the sea.

He'd have run down that hillside so fast
sun on the waves bounced him to us,
out of the camp's ditches, causeways,
axes and bones, to the foxholes and rat runs

of Whitehawk where friends he outpaced
one spring afternoon are still calling
five thousand years on. Re-united, they climb
to the grandstand. They move through racks

of fake Adidas, gold bracelets, the shove
and fried onions of a bank holiday market
the way flint or a necklace, the rim of a pot,
will find a path up through the earth.

Cuckmere Haven

The turf's knitted with violets,
viola hirta, odourless, penitent.

The larks that hide here,
singing for their lovers,

spin everything that's ever been said
between her and him,

the great tangled mess of 16 years,
into a rope of conchylian purple

that she tightens round her fists,
hooks round an ankle, winching her

away from neatly paired walkers
trampling cowslips in sheep fields,

and away from the looped,
confused old river,

its swans, paddling in the lazy flow,
so achingly monogamous.

Suspended

Earth enters this house of sleep
to redeem it, call in the loan.
It brings picks, hunger pangs;
cups and bracelets cradled in clay.

The future's in the house too,
at the kitchen table, planning itself
into cells that renew or multiply
until sleep's clapped away by hooves –

a pony owned by the man at the top
of our hill. He's sitting tall in a cart,
stepping both of them out to the Downs,
hundreds of criss-crossing paths.

Improvisation
(for Alastair)

"Fear not the future, weep not for the past."
Percy Bysshe Shelley, *The Revolt of Islam Canto XI*

Just as a wave is never the same
and a horizon's always changed
by the passage of people and icebergs,

just as the city crumbles and grows,
knitting each language it holds
into another like a perfect dawn,

just as presidents come and go
on the same endlessly rolled
red carpet, to the same applause,

you might step into a hesitation
of the clock where the boy you were
at seventeen is wiping sweat from a violin,

as an older you brushes paper
from white to green. The body leads
each of us to water, to one another.

Let tomorrow always be a scale,
the taste of unfamiliar fruit, the sky –
an unrepeatable, maverick display,

let tomorrow lead to the docks
where anyone may arrive or disappear,
leaving sand, a dropped note, lost watch,

let tomorrow be an unmissable ballet
of eyes, hands, feet, the brass
of voices, a cello in the hum of play.

Where I live

I'll walk you to town,
in winter serious with conferences and church outings,
in summer, a rainbow of Pride.

We might see Tony and Fred discussing redheads
at a café in the North Laines.
Here are shops selling fifties dresses,
the one that rescues old leather sofas,
a homeopath smelling of lavender and grapefruit.

To the Pavilion gardens where Gareth plays sax,
mousy dreadlocks to his waist, brushing the rosemary
as he moves to Miles or Coltrane.

And the Pavilion itself
where the Prince Regent scoffed his mistress
while stones shattered the glass.

Pass the Theatre Royal, aching to be so camp,
to streets of fishermen's homes
where Russian and Twi mix in the twittens
and flint walls answer in Urdu or Japanese
all the way to the beach.

We'll stand for a moment
in the heat of a pavement, blast of north wind.

To the left, Palace Pier, its sentimental helter skelter,
to the right the West Pier's ribs are bare now,
a reminder of Aids, the three months of waiting, the test.

You know about the starlings, but before they fly,
let's go down past the Peter Pan playground
to a floating Chinese restaurant,
listen to them sing to the slap of rigging.

This is the Marina, its wall designed by a woman
who curved concrete like a coracle skin.

We'll pass shrubs where married men cruise,
follow a road where boys polish their Vauxhalls for racing.

On our way back to the prom, by the Old Ship Hotel
see the world with a hole in, the 'Donut',
on the wall of every student from Germany to Nigeria
who ever peered through, smiling to camera

and there's the kissing statue, its tilting heads of lovers
paired like snatched weekends,
through which the sea glances, maybe roars.

II

A bike ride to Shoreham,
ignoring the signs, cold, easterly wind,
you come to a fishmonger and the Babylon Lounge,
where one night a month
Kanda's in his sapeur's clothes,
stylish grandfather, tunes in his hands,

down to the lagoon, flat-bottomed dinghies,
so shallow, a safe place to learn.

Arrive at the end of the wide promenade
where beach huts dare the waves to enter,
where railings tail off at a mock lighthouse
and the harbour begins with homes of the famous,
Zoe and Heather, Fat Boy, once Paul,
a newspaper man, with their own private playgrounds.

Into the docks now, to cement works, wood yards,
the mountains of shingle, small hidden cafe.

Here are the cormorants, cars parked for sleep, moments of quiet.

Spot the tankers, attempt to speak the unpronounceable names,
enter the kingdom of ballast, sand, steel and freight,
of cranes and of fish, the stop and the go, the locks and the water,
vast gates measuring sea by the mark it makes.

From here to the coast road, traffic chicaned into two lanes –
inadequate pavement, inadequate kerbs.
A tunnel of dust and shavings, of litter and dirt,
scrap yard and sheds. You wobble between lorry and lorry,
each twinned wheel shaking you to mud-cradled houseboats
and a Piper lands at the airport.

You make your way to a shingle drift, its sea cabbage, its kites.

III

Or we could trek across to the allotments on the flint ridge,
find scrapers and Bongo's old shed, his chickens, the parties and flags,
cats hiding in couch grass. Hear the man with a trumpet,
watch the swapping of seeds and stories of badgers
knocking down the ripe maize. A dog fox'll surprise you,
the magpies will gossip and if you look up there'll be yachts in the distance

Drop down a rutted track, leaving the racecourse behind,
to the hospital where my aunt gave up her breath
to a cubical drawn around night and I took my unanswered goodbye
back past a spur of the Downs, feeling her stiff, impossible steps,

to Queen's Park afternoons spent in a sandpit, the give of a swing,
lurch of a seesaw, skirting Hanover's terraces,
where for the price of a fare you can ride a roller coaster,
teeter down Southover on top of a bus, past the Greys,
and the Geese, the pub with no name.

But tonight, back to my own hill, a slow amble down,
Vera's old meadows long filled in,
Louis' ears deaf to the train that once rumbled to Kemp Town.
On the other side of the cemetery Brendan is writing
or watching the trees. I stand at the door, look up to the workhouse
now turned into wards for the old and confused, for the mentally ill,
that woke us one night as it crackled from a fire in the laundry,
the skyline ragged with smoke and flames.

A full moon is rising out of the elms and I think of my neighbours,
of Justine and Fi, of Nick and Julie, of Quentin and Sophie

and how in summer our street is a door, always open,
how in winter the lights signal whether we're home,
how my apple tree blossoms so briefly but bows to us all.

IV

It's a march back in time to the Concorde,
its history unwritten, replaced by limestone terraces
for Burger King, an amusement arcade.

The jazz that played here has gone back to the sea
or soaked into the aquarium behind,
with the conversations between exiles
about Robben Island, tending weeds between cracks
just for the closeness of leaves. Conversations remaindered
like stripes on a book transferred to a turtle's shell,
the turn of a seahorse's head, kept alive in the near dark,
in habitats mimicked behind glass.

On the Concorde's small stage, music grappled with fame,
enthusiasts silent for piano, tenor sax, the hi hat and the bass.
We squeezed into spaces on circular tables, Jane and I, before children,
when it lifted itself up and crawled down the front,
past colonnades preserved from the storms in Brighton green,
to stop near the lift where rock replaced jazz,
an old reggae name for old times. The new exiles belong to different regimes.

On the beach ridges of seaweed are patterned with wood,
planks from a cargo lost in a gale, forked branches of trees,
a green apple and rope. Magnolia-front flats rise from the coast road
to the sun and the pier radio ebbs on the wind.

Spinnakers tilt on the horizon, quick brush strokes, parentheses.
And in these brackets live Jama, his jazz gone to the coffin,
and all who went home remembering the release from lager and heat,
the exit to applause of pebbles and waves,
the place where they halted, spent a few years,
Mbeki among them, replaced by Sudanese, Ugandans,
thin men from Zim, who will the horizon to fold itself up,
to enclose them and see them home safe.

Biographical note

JACKIE WILLS' first collection, *Powder Tower* (Arc, 1995), was shortlisted for the 1995 T.S. Eliot prize and was a PBS Recommendation. In 2004, *Mslexia* magazine named her one of the top 10 new women poets of the decade. She was poet in residence at the Aldeburgh Poetry Festival in 2004 and has worked with orchestras, museums, galleries and visual artists.

Recent titles in Arc Publications'
POETRY FROM THE UK / IRELAND,
edited by Jo Shapcott, include:

LIZ ALMOND
The Shut Drawer

JONATHAN ASSER
Outside The All Stars

DONALD ATKINSON
In Waterlight: Poems New, Selected & Revised

JOANNA BOULTER
*Twenty Four Preludes & Fugues on
Dmitri Shostakovich*

THOMAS A CLARK
The Path to the Sea

TONY CURTIS
What Darkness Covers
The Well in the Rain

JULIA DARLING
Sudden Collapses in Public Places
Apology for Absence

CHRIS EMERY
Radio Nostalgia

KATHERINE GALLAGHER
Circus-Apprentice

CHRISSIE GITTINS
Armature

MICHAEL HASLAM
The Music Laid Her Songs in Language
A Sinner Saved by Grace

JOEL LANE
Trouble in the Heartland

TARIQ LATIF
The Punjabi Weddings